THE OFFICIAL WEST BROMWICH ALBION ANNUAL 2012

Written by Dave Bowler

Designed by Brian Thomson

A Grange Publication

Printed in the EU.

Photography by Laurie Rampling, AMA Sports Photography & Dave Bowler

ISBN: 978-1-908221-38-4

£7.99

WEST BROMWICH
ALBION

cOnTenTS

rOy of thE AlbiON

Yes, we know it's supposed to be Roy of the Rovers, but we're not changing our name after 130 years, not even for Roy Hodgson!

But if anybody could cause us to think again about our name, it would be Albion's head coach because there have been few people in Albion's history who have made such a big impact in such a short space of time.

When Hodgson joined us in early February, it looked as if the Throstles were doomed to live up to our yo-yo tag once again as we dropped down the league table after our stunning start to the season.

But by bringing in the ancient principles of organisation, hard work and a strong team spirit, Roy brought the very best out of our talented team, quickly shaking off any fears of a return to the Championship and giving us some amazing days against Liverpool, Villa, Sunderland, Everton and Newcastle along the way.

By the end of it all, we weren't thinking about the drop, but cursing our luck at finishing just a place short of the top half – how's that for a turnaround!?

The big challenge now is to repeat that late season form over the course of 38 Premier League games, to keep Albion in the top flight and to achieve the biggest hat-trick of all – a third consecutive season in the top division. If anyone can, Roy can!

Build a rOckEt bOYs...

Records tumbled, big names were humbled, reputations stumbled and goalkeepers fumbled, may the Lord forever bless Edwin van der Sar in his retirement.

We saw monumental displays, against-the-odds results, champagne football and bread and butter grinds. Some will linger long in the memory, others just staging posts on the way to the real goal – surviving!

MICHAEL APPLETON

"Going into the season we were quietly confident we could get rid of the tag as a yo-yo club and retain our status. Having had a year in this league before, the likes of Jonas Olsson, Chris Brunt, James Morrison, Youssouf Mulumbu were all better for it. They knew what was coming."

PAUL SCHARNER

"We are a young squad with big potential, as you can see at the end of the season. For young players, they are learning, it is hard to be consistent, so you need some experienced players around them if you are going to be successful. We have a good mix."

MICHAEL APPLETON

"Possibly the defeat at Chelsea was a good thing. If you are going to get thumped, the opening day is as good a time as any! It was a wake up call, a reminder of the standards in this division, that you make a mistake and it gets punished. We needed to put things right and we did the following week with a win and a clean sheet against Sunderland."

PETER ODEMWINGIE

"I watched the 6-0 game against Chelsea on TV with friends in London because I had signed but the paperwork was not done at that point. Even with the score, I was impressed with some periods of play, I thought the team had quality and I thought I could add things to it. I knew it would be OK!

I trained one day in the week up to Sunderland. I was processing my work permit, trained on Friday, Saturday I started my career and it started with a winning goal. It was a beautiful day, the supporters were wonderful and I was very happy straight away. Even during the warm up, I felt they had confidence in me and that was very nice. The goal against Sunderland is my favourite for the season. It was the winner, in the last minutes, and it was my first for the club, on my debut, so personally it was very important too."

PAUL SCHARNER

"My opinion is that the big teams, as we say in Austria, they also cook with water! They are only 11 players like us, they don't have any other ingredients, so you should not be afraid of them. So in the changing room before the game against Arsenal at the Emirates, I said to the players, "Come on, let's go and pick up the three points". People say this is a change in the psychology of the club compared with previous seasons, so I hope that is something I have been able to add here from my own experience. At this high level, it is the mentality that can give you the few extra per cent that can be the difference between teams."

JONAS OLSSON

"The first three months of the season were a true joy, a great atmosphere in the dressing room and around the club. I think we have stepped up a long way as we saw at Arsenal and Manchester United, because there was perhaps more belief in the team that we could do well there, and we felt we belonged. The character of the side is very important and you saw that at Old Trafford, to come from 2-0 down to draw, and be the only team to get points at Old Trafford this season. Being a United fan growing up, it was a highlight of the season."

PETER ODEMWINGIE

"Games where you don't expect to pick up points but at the end of the 90 minutes you come out with a smile – they are important, they boost your morale and the game against Arsenal was that way. Those things mean, all season, you feel that no matter who the opponent is, you can get some points. Scoring at the Emirates Stadium was nice because there are a lot of Arsenal supporters in Nigeria so I made a name for myself!"

MICHAEL APPLETON

"Blackpool away turned into a nightmare but it wasn't a bad performance, even with the nine men. It took us a while to get over that defeat and you can't afford to have a hangover from a result in this league because a lot of points can get away from you if you do. The fact we used up so much energy on the night, it knocked the stuffing out of us a bit, and mentally, we felt it was a missed opportunity to get some good points. But at the end of November, we won at Everton, beat Newcastle and that catapulted us back up the league so there were no alarm bells ringing.

You saw the fine line between success and failure in this division over Christmas where we played pretty well, especially at Bolton and against Manchester United, but we lost all four games in just over a week and then you do start to fear for the team a little bit. United summed up that period, we played great, the ref missed a stonewall penalty, they should have been down to ten, we missed a penalty, that was how things were going for us. It was a tough spell, we couldn't get going again and, in the end, that was what led to the departure of Robbie."

PETER ODEMWINGIE

“It was very difficult when Roberto Di Matteo left because he was the coach that brought me here. I’m very grateful to him for bringing me to the Premier League and for giving me the confidence I needed. All those things matter very much to a player. I was in a mood for a couple of weeks after he left, I found it very difficult to forget it and move on. Of course, you have to then impress the new coach, training became more intense, but maybe I was not in a good frame of mind so it was a slow start for me. But you get over it, new feelings came in, I enjoyed working with Roy Hodgson and I enjoy being here, so I got my chance to start a game, I did well, and he has shown a lot of confidence in me which I’m grateful for.”

JONAS OLSSON

“Roy Hodgson is well known at home, he’s a semi-Swede, had a great record there, one of the top coaches ever in Swedish football. The Swedish press have always followed his progress around the world so I knew a few things about him before he came in. He is very impressive to work with, a good coach and a good person. His experience and knowledge made us believe again and we have got some tremendous results since then. We have a very professional locker room, players are here to win, so they will work hard to achieve that. The statistics that show how often we have come from behind show we have a never-say-die attitude and those things together have been very important.”

ROY HODGSON

“I think we were among the favourites to be relegated when I joined. We were on the slide and people expect it to continue. It’s a great credit to the players that they were able to pull out of that and recapture the form and the belief they had earlier in the season when they were getting great results and playing very well.

When you select your first few teams, you’re not as confident as you’d like to be because you don’t really know enough, the players are finding out what it is I expect, and so the fighting spirit I found here was extremely important because it was a very good starting point. Looking back, the late goal we scored against Wolves to get a draw was very important in starting the ball rolling. It was an equaliser our pressure deserved and it became something of a turning point.”

MICHAEL APPLETON

"Against Wolves, we stayed in the game, Carlos took his opportunity and that was a pivotal moment because it gave us great momentum going on from there, it gave us a platform and some belief which we then took to Stoke, did the same again and from there, the players could see the value of what the gaffer was asking them to do. We've been more compact, we're better out of possession, and we've been harder to break down, without losing that cutting edge, the ability to play good attacking football."

ROY HODGSON

"There were some fine performances against Birmingham. We were possibly fortunate to catch them at the right time, just after they'd won the League Cup, and when they had one or two injuries. But if you get that bit of fortune, you must take advantage of it and the players did that extremely well, we were the better team on the day, and it was an important staging point. Birmingham don't lose many at home so it was very good for confidence. The breaks in March where there was an FA Cup weekend and then an international break gave us a little more time to work with players on the organisation of the team and they responded very quickly. They're an intelligent group, they wanted to succeed, they wanted to get the results, and their application has been very good."

JONAS OLSSON

"The Liverpool game was special for everyone. I had some friends here from Sweden and they were Liverpool fans so it meant a lot to me to win! I'm sure it was special for the gaffer, that's natural, but most important, we played very well, deserved to win and it took us away from relegation and gave us breathing space from the bottom which was important."

PAUL SCHARNER

"The focus was on the defensive shape, we concede too many goals and you can see the changes he has made. We don't have many clean sheets, but it helps if you only concede one goal! Training is very tactical, we are very focused on the shape, on one-on-one situations, but we are still a good offensive team too and we score many goals. Sunderland was a good example, a fantastic team performance that shows that we know what you need to stay in this division."

MICHAEL APPLETON

"What was pleasing after Liverpool was going up to Sunderland and doing it again, getting the three points and making those Liverpool points stick, because it's easy to have a little bit of 'after the Lord Mayor's show' following a victory like that. We weren't great first half – didn't do too much wrong, but weren't asking many questions. It was great to watch the gaffer because he really showed his experience that day. I remember wondering if he was going to get after the players at half-time at 2-1 down, but he was very calm, very quiet, told them they were doing well, that they were getting better as the game went on, told them they'd win the game and how they'd do it, and ultimately they did. Those are great lessons to learn."

ROY HODGSON

“We went into the Aston Villa game without Brunt, Reid and Thomas, then Jara at half time too. We conceded early on, Scharner then got sent off, but the team is prepared to go to the end of the game, go the last mile, and once again it paid off and with three games to spare, we no longer had any worries in terms of our prospects for next season which is a wonderful feeling.”

PAUL SCHARNER

“The last third of the season is the most important, that is where the decisions are made and it is important to be in good shape for this point in time, and to be very focused. As a team, we have played some of our best and most successful football in this period and that is why we are safe in the league now.”

ROY HODGSON

“The atmosphere here is as good as anything I’ve ever experienced and that is testimony to the supporters’ appreciation of the game and of the football club and I hope that continues for years to come. I think we’re fortunate that we have fans who value the club, value the history, value what we’ve done and what we stand for as a club and who understand that consistently having a place in the top 20 is not a failure as some see it, but a success within the context of the modern game.”

PETER ODEMWINGIE

“The goal against Villa was a good one for a striker, it needed quick reactions in the six-yard area. It was a little like the goal away at Sunderland where you just need to be quickest to the ball, where you have to smell where the ball is coming to and then be there. I’m very happy to score goals like that one, they’re not the most beautiful but they are as important to the team as one from 30 yards. They are about instinct and intuition.”

SeASOn sTatS:

Date	Opposition	Score	Scorers
Sat, Aug 14	Chelsea	0-6	
Sat, Aug 21	SUNDERLAND	1-0	Odemwingie
Tue, Aug 24	Leyton Orient (CC2)	2-0	Ibanez, Wood
Sun, Aug 29	Liverpool	0-1	
Sat, Sep 11	TOTTENHAM HOTSPUR	1-1	Brunt
Sat, Sep 18	BIRMINGHAM CITY	3-1	Olsson, Odemwingie, own goal
Wed, Sep 22	MANCHESTER CITY (CC3)	2-1	Cox, Zuiverloon
Sat, Sep 25	Arsenal	3-2	Odemwingie, Jara, Thomas
Sat, Oct 2	BOLTON WANDERERS	1-1	Morrison
Sat, Oct 16	Manchester United	2-2	Tchoyi, own goal
Sat, Oct 23	FULHAM	2-1	Fortune, Mulumbu
Tues, Oct 26	Leicester City (CC4)	4-1	Cox 2, Reid, Tchoyi
Mon, Nov 1	Blackpool	1-2	Mulumbu
Sun, Nov 7	MANCHESTER CITY	0-2	
Wed, Nov 10	West Ham United	2-2	Odemwingie, Ibanez
Sat, Nov 13	Wigan Athletic	0-1	
Sat, Nov 20	STOKE CITY	0-3	
Sat, Nov 27	Everton	4-1	Scharner, Brunt, Tchoyi, Mulumbu
Wed, Dec 1	Ipswich Town (CC5)	0-1	
Sun, Dec 5	NEWCASTLE UNITED	3-1	Odemwingie 2, Tchoyi
Sat, Dec 11	Aston Villa	1-2	Scharner
Sun, Dec 26	Bolton Wanderers	0-2	
Tue, Dec 28	BLACKBURN ROVERS	1-3	Thomas
Sat, Jan 1	MANCHESTER UNITED	1-2	Morrison
Tue, Jan 4	Fulham	0-3	
Sat, Jan 8	Reading (FAC3)	0-1	
Sat, Jan 15	BLACKPOOL	3-2	Odemwingie 2, Morrison
Sun, Jan 23	Blackburn Rovers	0-2	
Tue, Feb 1	WIGAN ATHLETIC	2-2	Odemwingie, Fortune
Sat, Feb 5	Manchester City	0-3	
Sat, Feb 12	WEST HAM UNITED	3-3	Dorrans, Thomas, own goal
Sun, Feb 20	WOLVERHAMPTON WANDERERS	1-1	Vela
Mon, Feb 28	Stoke City	1-1	Vela
Sat, Mar 5	Birmingham City	3-1	Morrison, Mulumbu, Scharner
Sat, Mar 19	ARSENAL	2-2	Odemwingie, Reid
Sat, Apr 2	LIVERPOOL	2-1	Brunt 2
Sat, Apr 9	Sunderland	3-2	Odemwingie, Mulumbu, Scharner
Sat, Apr 16	CHELSEA	1-3	Odemwingie
Sat, Apr 23	Tottenham Hotspur	2-2	Odemwingie, Cox
Sat, Apr 30	ASTON VILLA	2-1	Odemwingie, Mulumbu
Sun, May 8	Wolverhampton Wanderers	1-3	Odemwingie
Sat, May 14	EVERTON	1-0	Mulumbu
Sun, May 22	Newcastle United	3-3	Tchoyi 3

Jonas is looking a bit confused – but looking at this wordsearch upside down isn't going to help!

See if you can help him find these 10 Albion words:

BAGGIE BIRD
BOAZ
BRUNT
DORRANS
GERA
MCAULEY
MULUMBU
ODEMWINGIE
REID
THROSTLES

M	U	L	U	M	B	U	D	O	I	T
C	S	U	V	A	O	A	U	R	F	H
A	R	G	E	R	A	D	D	A	V	R
U	H	B	G	I	Z	N	O	Z	L	O
L	Q	R	Z	Q	Y	X	R	M	Y	S
E	K	E	O	K	O	B	R	U	N	T
Y	B	I	B	A	W	H	A	M	S	L
G	O	D	E	M	W	I	N	G	I	E
S	F	I	J	M	L	F	S	G	O	S
J	E	T	J	R	P	Y	C	T	U	E
B	A	G	G	I	E	B	I	R	D	Z

Answers on Page 61

Mapping it Out

The current flock of Throstles have migrated to The Hawthorns from all kinds of places.

To honour their journey, here's an Albion map of Europe – see where your favourite player has come from!

JONAS OLSSON
• *Sweden* •

GRAHAM DORRANS
• *Scotland* •

MARC-ANTOINE FORTUNE
• *France* •

CHRIS BRUNT
• *Northern Ireland* •

PABLO IBANEZ
• *Spain* •

JEROME THOMAS
England

GABRIEL
TAMAS
• Romania •
PAUL
SCHARNER
• Austria •
MAREK
CECH
• Slovakia •

Somen Tchoyi

First professional game

I was playing in Norway for Odd Grenland in 2005. We played against Tromso. I started but was quite nervous even though I knew in the lead up to the game, I'd be involved. It was my first year playing football in Europe.

First professional goal

I was still at Odd Grenland away against Lyn Oslo. One of our players crossed the ball but the defender hit it back into play. I took one touch to the right and I curled it into the net. I just ran off, in celebration.

First kit

It was a Marseille shirt in light and dark blue. I loved them so I bought the shirt.

First player you swapped shirts with

It was when I played in the Europa League with Red Bull Salzburg. I swapped with Senna playing for Villareal. He was a player I had admired for a long time and had watched him play from home when I was younger. I don't swap shirts very often.

First significant injury

I damaged my Achilles tendon in a friendly game for Stabaek and I was supposed to be out for a month but I was only out for about three weeks in the end. It was painful though.

First-ever room-mate in your professional career

It was Olivier Occean, when we were both at Odd Grenland. He's Canadian and now plays in Germany. We don't see each other very often but stay in touch by email.

pAint A MAn!

No wonder Steven Reid looks fed up – somebody's pinched the colours off his shirt!

Put a bit of colour back in his cheeks by designing a new Albion shirt for him!

the ReCOrd BREaKerS

If you want to know the biggest, the best, the worst and the most expensive in Albion history, this is the place to find out – all our records are here!

Borja Valero

RECORD SIGNING:
£4,700,000 from Real Mallorca, August 2008

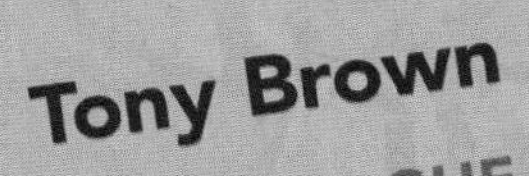

Tony Brown

RECORD CAREER LEAGUE GOALSCORER:
218, from 1963-1981

RECORD CAREER GOALSCORER IN ALL GAMES:
279

RECORD CAREER LEAGUE APPEARANCES:
574 (561 and 13 sub)

RECORD CAREER APPEARANCES IN ALL GAMES:
720 (706 and 14 sub)

RECORD POINTS TOTAL (3 PTS):
91 in FL Championship, 2009/10

Curtis Davies

RECORD TRANSFER RECEIVED:
£8,500,000 from Villa, July 2008

RECORD SEASONAL LEAGUE GOALSCORER:
WG Richardson, 39 in 1935/36

BIGGEST LEAGUE WIN:
12-0 vs Darwen (h), April 4, 1892

BIGGEST FA CUP WIN:
10-1 vs Chatham (a), March 2, 1889

BIGGEST LEAGUE CUP WIN:
6-1 vs Coventry City (h), 1965/66 and 6-1 vs Aston Villa (h), 1966/67

BIGGEST LEAGUE DEFEAT:
10-3 vs Stoke City (a), February 4, 1937

BIGGEST FA CUP DEFEAT:
5-0 vs Leeds United (a), February 18, 1967

BIGGEST LEAGUE CUP DEFEAT:
6-1 vs Nottingham Forest, October 6, 1982

BIGGEST LEAGUE ATTENDANCE:
60,945 vs Wolves, March 4, 1950

BIGGEST ATTENDANCE:
64,815 vs Arsenal, March 6, 1937

LOWEST ATTENDANCE:
1,050 vs Sheffield United, April 30, 1901

RECORD POINTS TOTAL (2 PTS):
60 in Division One, 1919/20

RECORD SEASONAL LEAGUE GOALS TOTAL:
105 in Division Two, 1929/30

MOST CAPPED PLAYER WHILE AT THE ALBION:
Stuart Williams, 33 for Wales

OLDEST PLAYER:
George Baddeley, 39 years, 345 days vs Sheffield Wednesday, April 18, 1914.

YOUNGEST PLAYER:
Frank Hodgetts, 16 years, 26 days vs Notts County, October, 1940.

WEST BROMWICH
ALBION

NEW PLAYER!

gAMe On fOr GareTh!

Central defender Gareth McAuley became Roy Hodgson's first signing for the club at the end of last season when he moved to The Hawthorns from Ipswich Town – and wasn't he delighted about it!

"I've tried to keep the feeling in - but I feel like a kid in a candy shop inside. It's a great thing to look forward to, to try to establish myself at this level."

It's Gareth's first chance to play in the Premier League after making his name in this country with Lincoln, Leicester and Ipswich.

"The gaffer told me he has seen me play a few times. He told me he was impressed and he wanted me to come here to work with him and develop my game. He has got such a wealth of knowledge and I think he'll improve me and that's all anyone wants to do.

"The club wants to move forward and cement itself in the Barclays Premier League on a permanent basis and become a top Premier League club. It's going to be hard to try and break into the team but that's my aim. I have enough faith in myself I can do that.

"I've played a lot of games in the Championship, which is a tough, tough division, as the players here will know. Teams have top strikers and I've played against that type of opposition week in, week out".

As the captain of Northern Ireland, Gareth already knows plenty about our skipper, Chris Brunt.

"Brunty has been here a while. He's a fans' favourite and skipper of the club. He's a great player and he's been a friend of mine for a few years.

"I didn't need to pick his brains too much about what the place was like. But he only had good things to say and that helped make my decision."

Gareth also knows Simon Cox, having come across him in an international last summer. As Coxy was on the winning side for the Republic of Ireland, he'll probably have already mentioned that to Gareth a few times!

FOOTBALL FIRSTS

gRAhaM DOrRanS

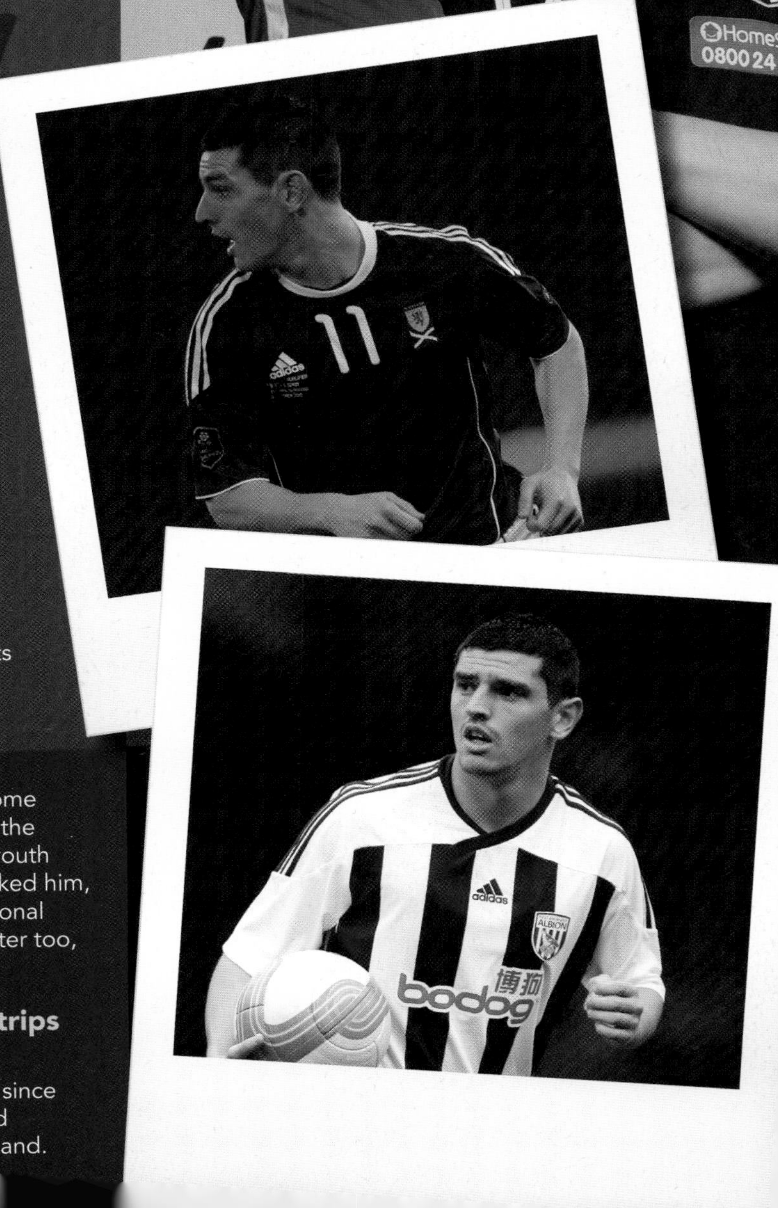

First professional game

Livingston against Hearts. I think we lost 2-1 and I was about 17. We were doing well but they equalised, then Roman Bednar came on and scored the winner for them. I started the game and was a bit nervous but was happy with my performance.

First red card...

It was the season before I came to Albion and it was our new manager's first game in charge. I got two yellow cards and one was for dissent so he wasn't very happy.

First kit

I got bought a Rangers shirt by my parents when I was a boy but it didn't have a name or number on it. The first shirt I bought that did was on a school trip to the Nou Camp. I got one with Rivaldo on the back - a week later, he left Barcelona!

First player you swapped shirts with

Barry Ferguson at Rangers. I was on the bench for Livingston and I got on for the last ten minutes or so, so I swapped shirts with him. He's another player I watched when I was growing up and admired.

First manager/coach

I've been lucky enough to work under some good people but the first one to stick in the memory was Alex Cleland – he was my youth team manager at Livingston. Everyone liked him, he got involved with everyone on a personal level and joined in with some of the banter too, so the players enjoyed that.

First-ever room-mate on away trips in your professional career

I've played alongside Robert Snodgrass since I was 13. He is at Leeds now but I played alongside him at club level and for Scotland.

tHE BiG QuiZ

We're in the Premier League again for the sixth season, so to celebrate, we've got a special quiz all about our first five years in the top division – see if you can keep us in the top 20 again!

1. Who were Albion's first ever Premier League opponents?
2. Who scored Albion's first Premier League goal?
3. Which goalkeeper was first to save a penalty for us in the Premier League?
4. Who scored our first penalty?
5. Who got Albion's first red card?
6. Which team were the first to be beaten by the Baggies?
7. Where did we get our first away win?
8. Which managers and head coaches have led Albion in this division?
9. We've scored two hat-tricks – who got them?
10. And against which opposition?

11 Our biggest win?

12. Our worst defeat?

13. Only one Albion man has scored against Liverpool in our first 10 games - who?

14. Who scored the goals when we beat Portsmouth on the last day of the Great Escape season?

15. Who got the winner in our first win over Aston Villa?

16. Who scored the Albion goal in Roy Hodgson's first game in charge?

17. We've beaten Arsenal twice – who scored in the 2-1 win at The Hawthorns?

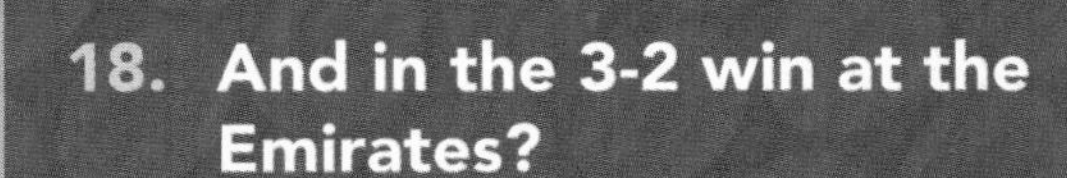

18. And in the 3-2 win at the Emirates?

19. We did three doubles last season – against which teams?

20. Who scored the first goal for us in 2010/11?

Answers on Page 61

LEFT-BACK: NEIL CLEMENT

A great Albion servant who played 300 games for the club, Clem's sweet left foot made him dangerous going forward, while as a defender, he could play on the left or at centre-half.

LEFT MIDFIELD CHRIS BRUNT

With his wand of a left foot, Chris is as good a crosser of the ball as there is anywhere in the Premiership, never mind at the Albion – he takes a mean free-kick as well!

CENTRE-HALF JONAS OLSSON

Albion's Super Swede has been a key player for the club in both of his Premier League campaigns so far. Albion's points per game record is way better when he plays than when he's been injured!

GOALKEEPER: TOMASZ KUSZCZAK

Our Pole in Goal wasn't at The Hawthorns for long before heading for Manchester United, but he made a big impression on the supporters before he left.

CENTRE-HALF DARREN MOORE

'Big Dave' is one of the great Albion cult heroes, such a legend that he already has a suite in The Hawthorns named in his honour. A giant of a man, and a giant with the fans!

RIGHT-BACK IGOR BALIS

The international man of mystery from Slovakia scored the all-important penalty at Bradford that got us into the Premiership the first time, and was an outstanding right-back once we were there.

RIGHT MIDFIELD ZOLTAN GERA

The Hungarian captain was quickly established as an Albion hero with a string of great goals and his tireless ability to chase up and down the right for the Baggies. It's good to have him back!

thE DReaM tEAm

THE PREMIER LEAGUE YEARS!

Plenty of players have represented the Baggies in our first five seasons in the Premier League. We've selected our all-time team from amongst them – who'd be in your team?

CENTRE MIDFIELD YOUSSOUF MULUMBU

Our reigning Player of the Year, Youssouf proved himself at Premier League last season with lots of busy performances and plenty of goals from the middle to boot. And he scored the winner against Villa!

STRIKER PETER ODEMWINGIE

Arriving almost unknown from Moscow, Peter soon made a name for himself with a string of match winning displays, ending the season as top scorer and only the second player to get to double figures in a Premiership season.

CENTRE MIDFIELD JONATHAN GREENING

The centrepiece of Tony Mowbray's Premiership team, Jonathan Greening was also the club captain and a huge influence on the team, either in the middle or as a winger.

STRIKER NWANKWO KANU

Completing an all Nigerian strike force, Kanu didn't play as many games as he should have for the Throstles, but when he was on the field, he scored his share of goals.

PLAYER OF THE SEASON

YOUSSOUF MULUMBU

He's Better Than Kaka!

He comes from Africa according to popular legend, and now he's won two awards that even Kaka hasn't managed!

Youssouf Mulumbu ran away with the votes as Albion's Player of the Season and the Players' Player of the Season, which was a bit on the greedy side, to be honest!

A typically modest Mulumbu said, "I'd like to thank my team-mates because without them I wouldn't have won these awards.

"The way the fans have supported me is a great thing. When they sing my name, it gives me a big boost. I'm very happy - but my work here isn't finished.

"There is a big pressure on me now because next season I have to improve and be an even better player to get even one trophy".

If he improves even more, we'll have to change the words to "better than Messi"!

MULUMBU
21

adidas
ALBION
bodog

ALBION
0800
247
999
HomeServe

BAck Of ThE NEt!

ALBION SCORED PLENTY OF GOALS LAST SEASON, AND SOME GREAT ONES TOO.

WE HAD NO SHORTAGE OF CHOICE WHEN WE CAME TO PICKING THE BEST OF THE LOT, THESE NINE MAKING OUR TOP TEN.

BUT THE WINNER? YOU'LL HAVE TO TURN THE PAGE...

247
999
HomeServe

Goals are what we crave and with the Throstles, goals are we get. Not many teams top the 50 mark in the Premier League, but we have, and there have been a few little beauties in amongst them. But Simon Cox served up the very best, late in the season at White Hart Lane to give us a 2-2 draw with Spurs and to win the BBC's "Goal of the Month" trophy to boot.

A little shimmy to create a yard of space, a swift glance to see a ball's width route to goal and a delicate stroke with the right foot to place the ball into a billowing net. But what did Simon make of it?

"Playing six or seven games in a row was great for me towards the end of the season, and scoring my first Premier League goal was a great moment for me personally. The main thing was that we got some good results during that period and that made sure we've got another chance at the Premier League again next season.

"The Spurs goal was very special, it was my first in the Premier League, my family were there to see it, and it was the start of a great day because I was staying in London to celebrate my birthday!"

gOaL Of ThE SeasOn

TOP SCORER: Peter Odemwingie

The Goal Machine!

To say Peter Odemwingie enjoyed a sensational introduction to the Premier League would be among the understatements of the season.

Only the second Albion man to reach double figures in a Premiership season, he surpassed Robert Earnshaw's 11 with something to spare and went on knocking in the goals, finishing with 15. And he won the Barclay's Premier League Player of the Month trophy twice to boot!

Often playing the lone striker role, his movement, strength, intelligence, raw pace and, most important, that rare goalscorer's instinct ensured Albion were always able to have the opposition guessing and always uncomfortable.

Peter's move to The Hawthorns was one of those times when everything just felt right, as he said at the end of the season: "It was a nice feeling from the start. The supporters welcomed me very quickly. I had a special feeling and after a season here, it feels as if I have been here a couple of years, I feel a big part of the club".

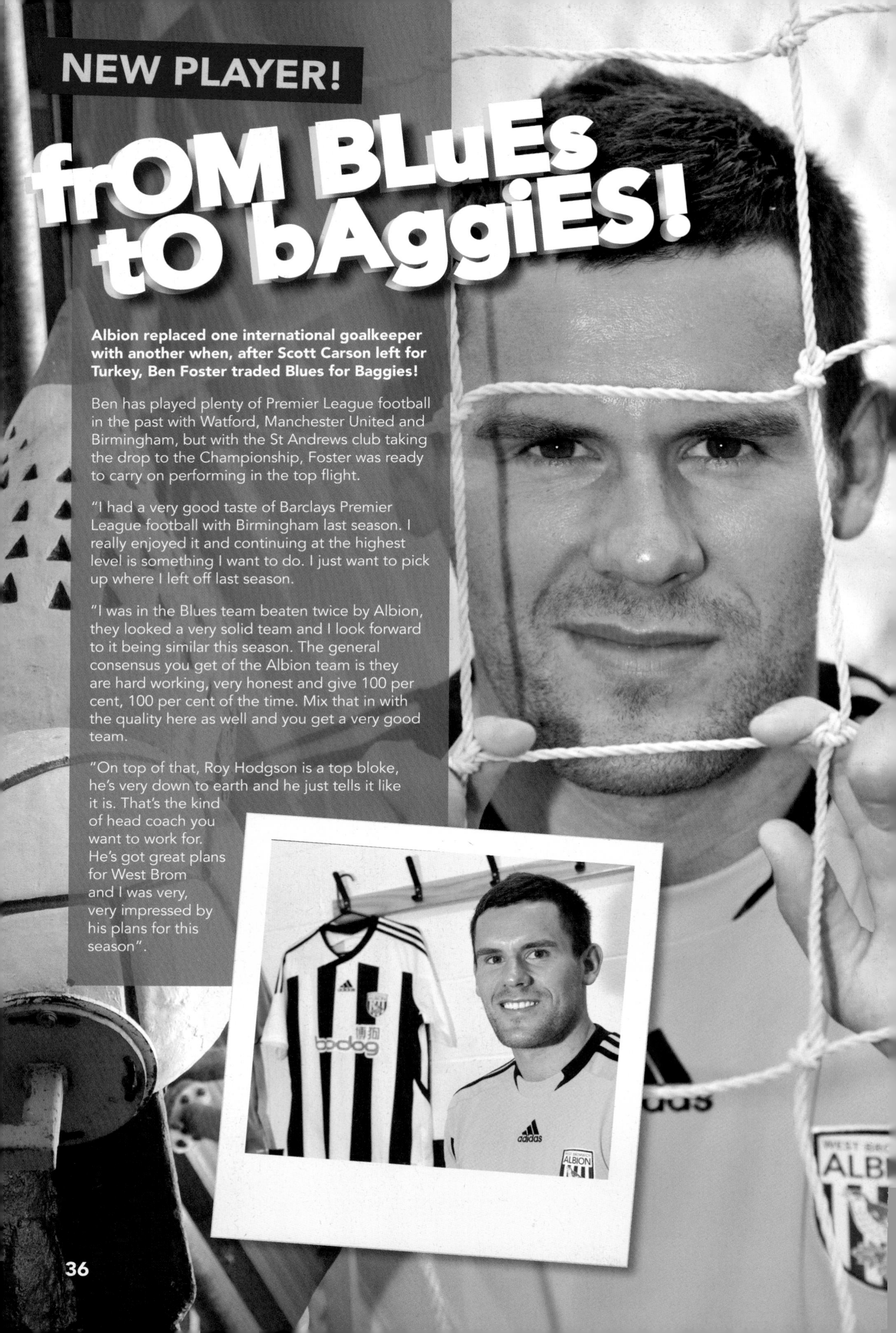

NEW PLAYER!

frOM BLuEs tO bAggiES!

Albion replaced one international goalkeeper with another when, after Scott Carson left for Turkey, Ben Foster traded Blues for Baggies!

Ben has played plenty of Premier League football in the past with Watford, Manchester United and Birmingham, but with the St Andrews club taking the drop to the Championship, Foster was ready to carry on performing in the top flight.

"I had a very good taste of Barclays Premier League football with Birmingham last season. I really enjoyed it and continuing at the highest level is something I want to do. I just want to pick up where I left off last season.

"I was in the Blues team beaten twice by Albion, they looked a very solid team and I look forward to it being similar this season. The general consensus you get of the Albion team is they are hard working, very honest and give 100 per cent, 100 per cent of the time. Mix that in with the quality here as well and you get a very good team.

"On top of that, Roy Hodgson is a top bloke, he's very down to earth and he just tells it like it is. That's the kind of head coach you want to work for. He's got great plans for West Brom and I was very, very impressed by his plans for this season".

FOOTBALL FIRSTS

JAMES MORRISON

First professional game

Notts County in the FA Cup for Middlesbrough and I was about 17 years old. I remember it was freezing cold and when I came on the score was 0-0. I didn't score that day but I know we scored two goals in two minutes to win the game. I had been told a few days before I would be on the bench so a lot of friends and family were there.

First professional goal

First round of the UEFA Cup for Boro, away at Banik Ostrava. It was my first full debut and I scored in the 90th minute. I was the first ever Boro player to score away in Europe and my goal was the equaliser that took us through to the next round. It was a special moment.

First red card

Against Manchester United away in the FA Cup at Old Trafford. Ronaldo was trying to do all his tricks and step-overs around me so the next time it happened I just kicked him to get at the ball. No arguments from me, I saw red really.

First kit

A Manchester United one with Ince's name and number on the back. My parents bought it for me when I was about six or seven. Two weeks later he left to join Inter Milan!

First player you swapped shirts with

Frank Lampard. I think it was my second Premier League game. I was on for the last 30 minutes. I try and get shirts from players I admire and who have done well in the game. I like to frame them.

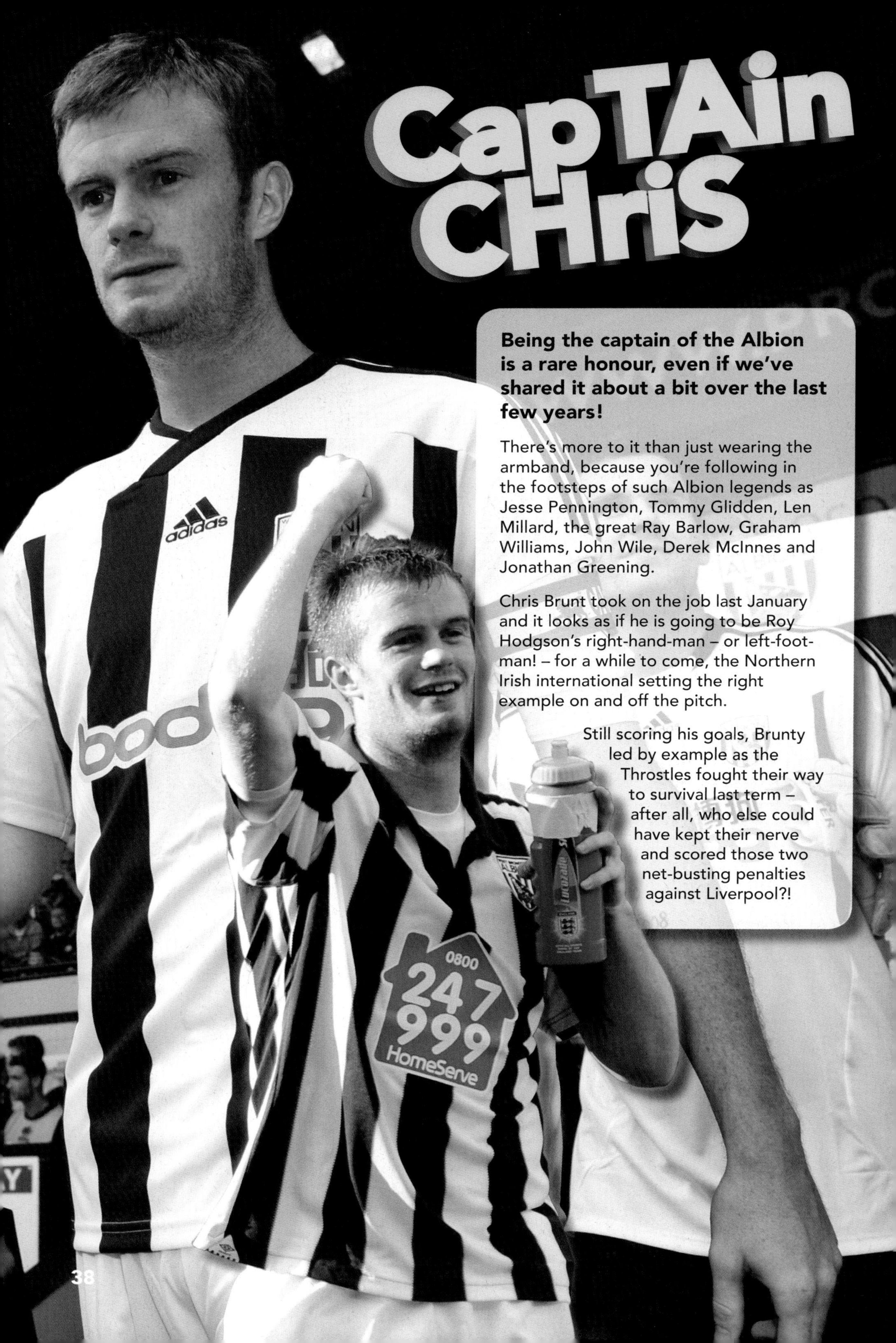

CapTAin CHriS

Being the captain of the Albion is a rare honour, even if we've shared it about a bit over the last few years!

There's more to it than just wearing the armband, because you're following in the footsteps of such Albion legends as Jesse Pennington, Tommy Glidden, Len Millard, the great Ray Barlow, Graham Williams, John Wile, Derek McInnes and Jonathan Greening.

Chris Brunt took on the job last January and it looks as if he is going to be Roy Hodgson's right-hand-man – or left-foot-man! – for a while to come, the Northern Irish international setting the right example on and off the pitch.

Still scoring his goals, Brunty led by example as the Throstles fought their way to survival last term – after all, who else could have kept their nerve and scored those two net-busting penalties against Liverpool?!

YOUNG PLAYER OF THE YEAR

JaMEs hUrSt

Albion's Academy has already shown signs that the long wait for some home grown players might soon be over.

We've seen Chris Wood, Sam Mantom and George Thorne make first team debuts in recent times, but just as impressive was James Hurst who was the deserving winner of the club's "Young Player of the Season" award.

James made his senior debut for Albion this term, setting a record unlikely to be beaten by playing his first three games in three different competitions: the League Cup, the Premier League and the FA Cup.

Back at The Hawthorns after a brief spell at Portsmouth, James noted: "The grass isn't always greener somewhere else!"

He'll be looking to force his way into the first team on a regular basis this season, so good luck to him!

NEW PLAYER!

tHe pROdiGaL sOn!

One of the nicest moments of last summer was the news that Zoltan Gera was coming back to The Hawthorns.

Zoltan made himself a big hero with the Albion fans the first time he was at the club, scoring loads of goals and creating even more, becoming a big part of the team that pulled off the Great Escape as well as being at the heart of the side that carried off the Football League Championship in 2008.

After four years as a Throstle, Gera moved to Fulham in the wake of that success, but we won't hold that against him! Because following three seasons at Craven Cottage, the Hungarian international realised that the grass is greener in the Black Country and came back to West Bromwich.

Welcome home, Zolly!

Jerome Thomas

First professional goal

It was a deflection against Spurs at White Hart Lane when I was at Charlton and I scored back at the Valley too. I think we won 3-1. I didn't celebrate much because it was a deflection but some of the boys came up and congratulated me.

First red card

Just after I joined Albion against Arsenal at the Emirates. I had an 'altercation' with Jack Wilshere, it got a bit heated and I got a straight red. I felt it was bit harsh, to be honest.

First kit

I remember having both Liverpool and Villa tops as a kid. My dad supported Villa in the '80s when they were doing well so that would have been my first. But I don't think I had anyone's name on the back. I had Thomas on the back of my Liverpool top though, which I got when I was a bit older.

First player you swapped shirts with

I only ever really swap shirts with old team mates as a rule. I have Thierry Henry's top from when Charlton played Arsenal, Ashley Cole's Chelsea top and then there's other players like Steve Sidwell, Darren Bent and Jermaine Pennant. There's been the odd occasion when I've got a top for a family member though, I have to admit.

First-ever room-mate in your professional career?

Jermaine Pennant when we played away for Arsenal in the Carling Cup. He and I are the same age. We get on well and are still in touch.

eWcaSTle oROwn DAy

It's traditional that for our final away game of the season, our fans get into party mode and turn up for a theme party.

We had the toga party in Twerton – ask your dad! – Vikings for Tommy Gaardsoe at Reading, superheroes for Super Kevin Phillips at QPR, and plenty of others down the years.

Last season, in honour of the local brew – ask your dad again! – we went to Newcastle to honour Mr Albion, Tony Brown, with a special Newcastle Brown Day!

Maskerade produced thousands of Tony Brown face masks depicting the great man as he looked in 1979, perm and all, and Albion fans throughout the ground wore them in his honour – the only Albion fan that didn't look like Tony Brown on the day was Bomber himself!

wHere AM i?

After James Morrison got a bang on the head against Arsenal last season, he didn't know where he was!

Help physio Richie Rawlins guide him back to the dressing room for treatment!

Answers on Page 61

uS aNd tHem

19 TEAMS FACE US IN THE BARCLAYS PREMIER LEAGUE THIS SEASON.

THESE ARE OUR BEST AND WORST RESULTS AGAINST THEM – HOPEFULLY SOME OF THE BEST ONES WILL GET EVEN BETTER THIS TERM. BUT LET'S NOT MAKE THE BAD ONES ANY WORSE!

Win: 7-0, 14 October 1922
Defeat: 2-6, 18 September 1970

ASTON VILLA:
Win: 7-0, 19 October 1936
Defeat: 1-7, 24 April 1899

BLACKBURN ROVERS:
Win: 8-1, 18 January 1936
Defeat: 2-6, 22 September 1888

BOLTON WANDERERS:
Win: 7-2, 8 December 1900
Defeat: 0-7, 7 December 1889

EVERTON:
Win: 6-1, 7 December 1935
Defeat: 1-7, 30 December 1893

FULHAM:
Win: 6-1, 24 November 1946
& 8 September 1962
Defeat: 1-6, 11 February 2006

MANCHESTER CITY:
Win: 9-2, 21 September 1957
Defeat: 1-7, 16 April 1938

NEWCASTLE UNITED:
Win: 7-3, 16 September 1953
Defeat: 1-5, 21 November 1931,
14 September 1938 & 26 November 1949

NORWICH CITY:
Win: 5-1, 18 December 1996
Defeat: 1-4, 21 November 1995

QUEENS PARK RANGERS:
Win: 5-1, 30 September 2007
Defeat: 1-3, 6 March 2010

STOKE CITY:
Win: 6-0, 18 December 1988
Defeat: 3-10, 4 February 1937

SUNDERLAND:
Win: 6-4, 27 February 1937
Defeat: 1-8, 22 October 1892

TOTTENHAM HOTSPUR:
Win: 5-0, 12 February 1927
Defeat: 0-5, 17 March 1951, 18 April 1959
& 28 November 1970

WIGAN ATHLETIC:
Win: 5-1, 24 April 1993
Defeat: 1-3, 2 October 2002

WOLVERHAMPTON WANDERERS:
Win: 8-0, 27 December 1893
Defeat: 0-7, 16 March 1963

Win: 6–3, 29 April 1968
Defeat: 0–7, 8 April 1970

Win: 6–2, 26 October 1929
Defeat: 1–6, 2 February 1929

Win: 5–2, 17 April 1929 & 24 October 1953
Defeat: 1–7, 3 December 1960

LIVERPOOL:

Win: 6-1, 1 December 1936
Defeat: 0-6, 26 April 2003

we WOn tHe CUp!

1888

In January 2012, we shall be embarking on yet another attempt to win the FA Cup.

It's always been a special competition to us and, with five FA Cup wins behind us, we're one of the competition's most successful clubs – in its 140-year history, only eight clubs have won it more often than we have, after all.

The first win came in 1888. Our opponents, Preston North End, were so confident they would win, they wanted to be photographed with the cup BEFORE kick-off! The referee refused, and just as well – we won 2-1, with goals from George Woodhall and Jem Bayliss.

We were the underdogs again in 1892 when we met Aston Villa in the final. But again the right side won – Albion were 3-0 winners which caused riots in Aston! Jasper Geddes, Sammy Nicholls and John Reynolds were on target and, to celebrate, we had the ball painted gold and a not so lucky dead throstle mounted on top of it!

1931

1892

1931

1954

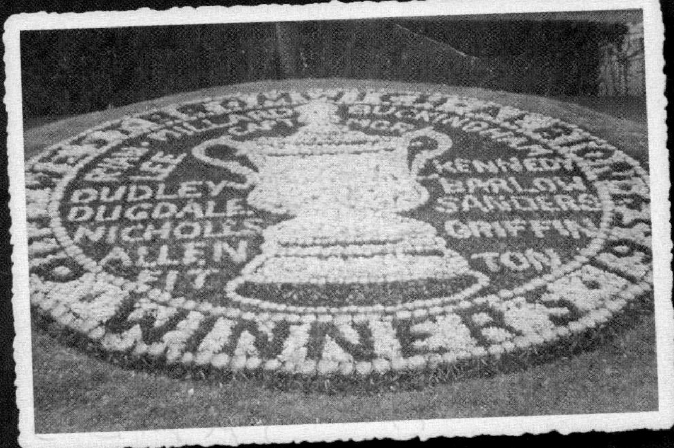

It was 1931 before we won the cup again, but that was our greatest triumph, when we became the first – and still the only – team to complete a unique double of winning the FA Cup and getting promoted in the same season. WG Richardson scored both goals as we beat Birmingham 2-1 in our first appearance at Wembley Stadium.

We almost did another double in 1954, but ended up second in the top flight. But we did carry off the FA Cup in great style, winning 3-2 over Preston North End, with Ronnie Allen scoring twice before Frank Griffin grabbed the late winner.

1954

1968

Our most recent victory came in 1968 when Jeff Astle scored that famous extra-time winner to defeat Everton with the only goal of the game.

All those cup winners became Albion immortals that will be remembered forever – do you fancy becoming the next generation of winners Brunty & co?!

1968

cROsswOrd

ACROSS:

1. Albion's kit manufacturer
5. Where do we play?
7. 11 Baggies make up a great what?
8. Scottish international Morrison's first name
11. The midfielder with blue hair
13. Our Welsh international goalie
15. Where did we sign Craig Dawson from?

DOWN:

1. West Bromwich ________
2. Famous former striker, ________ Goodman
3. Nicky is our left-back
4. On first name terms with our Hungarian star
6. Don't be formal with Mr Tchoyi
9. The skipper's first name
10. Michael ________ is our assistant head coach
11. He got our goal of last season
12. Which country does Gabriel Tamas come from?
14. Nationality of our former midfielder Richard Sneekes

Answers on Page 61

FOOTBALL FIRSTS

STEVEN REID

First professional game

It was the 1997/98 season, the last game of the season for Millwall. Tim Cahill and I got our debuts against Bournemouth at the Den under Billy Bonds. I'd just turned 17 and I was quite nervous. The pitch got invaded by fans with about ten minutes to go so my debut was cut short but it was still a proud moment for me.

First professional goal

For Millwall a couple of seasons later, away at Notts County. I was about 19 and it was in the good old days when I was a 'flying' winger. I cut inside the defender, took it wide and drilled a low shot which went in. The keeper should've saved it really! It was the worst celebration ever – I went over and shook the nearest player's hand – very old fashioned and formal. I got a bit of stick for that!

First kit

It was one of the old Wimbledon shirts. I was born and bought up in Kingston so my dad took me to Plough Lane a lot. I remember the shirt being wrapped up under the Christmas tree that year and I was convinced it was a box of chocolates so I went mad when I opened it and it was a Wimbledon kit. I was very proud of that.

First player you swapped shirts with

My first one was when I made my international debut against Croatia. I can't remember whose shirt it was but it was when I was still with Millwall. We weren't allowed to swap shirts at Millwall back then. I'll swap one if I play against a mate or get a decent result in a game, but I don't do it as a matter of course.

First significant injury

I've broken a toe and had hamstring injuries but the first biggie was only about three and a half years ago when I did the cruciate ligament in my knee. It kept me out for about seven months – nearly a whole season. I knew as soon as I'd done it, it was something really serious so I was prepared for the lay-off period. These days though the surgery for it is so good you can go straight into your rehab training the day after the op.

WEST BROM PLAYER PROFILES

LUKE DANIELS

POSITION: Goalkeeper

BIRTHDATE: 5/1/88

NATIONALITY: English

ALBION APPEARANCES: 0

ALBION GOALS: 0

Luke has been involved with the Albion since 2004 when he joined us from Manchester United. The young goalkeeper has yet to make a first team appearance for the Throstles but has racked up plenty of games when out on loan at clubs such as Shrewsbury Town, Tranmere Rovers, Rochdale and Motherwell. A season-long loan to Bristol Rovers fell through last season when he picked up a back injury, but now fully fit, he'll be looking to push Ben Foster this season.

STEVEN REID

POSITION: Full-back

BIRTHDATE: 10/3/81

NATIONALITY: Irish

ALBION APPEARANCES: 27+10

ALBION GOALS: 3

Steven has been an important member of the Albion squad since joining, initially on loan, towards the end of the 2009/10 promotion season. Mainly playing at right-back, Steven can also play in the midfield or at centre-half. He started out at Millwall, but also played a lot of Premier League football with Blackburn Rovers as well as being an Irish international. His experience in the game was vital as Albion secured another season in the top division.

GONZALO JARA

POSITION: Full-back

BIRTHDATE: 29/8/85

NATIONALITY: Chilean

ALBION APPEARANCES: 49+9

ALBION GOALS: 2

Gonzalo Jara enjoyed a very competitive fight with Steven Reid for the right-back position in the Albion team through last season. It was a mixed first season in the Premier League for the Chilean international who didn't get much time to rest up and prepare for it after representing his home country in the 2010 World Cup in South Africa. He was busy again last summer – this time in the Copa America!

NICKY SHOREY

POSITION: Full-back

BIRTHDATE: 19/2/81

NATIONALITY: English

ALBION APPEARANCES: 27+4

ALBION GOALS: 0

Nicky was an early season buy from Aston Villa last term and he and Marek Cech spent all season slugging it out between them at left-back. Nicky has played plenty of Premier League football in the past, notably with Reading before his move to Villa, while he also had a spell with Roy Hodgson on loan at Fulham. Nicky was a model of consistency and, like Steven Reid, his experience was so important to Albion as they secured Premiership survival.

JONAS OLSSON

POSITION: Centre-half

BIRTHDATE: 10/3/83

NATIONALITY: Swedish

ALBION APPEARANCES: 101+1

ALBION GOALS: 9

Jonas proved just how important a player he is for the Albion last season by being injured! When he missed games through November and December, Albion's good start to the season faltered, but once the giant guitar-playing defender returned to the team, the Throstles quickly got back on track. Also establishing himself as a Swedish international, the £800,000 he cost was money well spent!

CRAIG DAWSON

POSITION: Centre-half

BIRTHDATE: 6/5/90

NATIONALITY: English

ALBION APPEARANCES: 0

ALBION GOALS: 0

Craig Dawson has enjoyed a meteoric rise over the last couple of years, since joining League Two Rochdale from non-league Radcliffe Borough in 2009. He was a big player in the side that won promotion a year later, signing for Albion almost immediately before rejoining Rochdale on loan. A dependable defender, he's also a threat in the other penalty area scoring 21 goals in 93 games for Rochdale.

PABLO IBANEZ

POSITION: Centre-half

BIRTHDATE: 3/8/81

NATIONALITY: Spanish

ALBION APPEARANCES: 12+2

ALBION GOALS: 2

It took a while for Pablo to settle in to life in England after his switch from Spain during the summer of 2010, but there was never any questioning his ability with the ball at his feet. The physical nature of the English game can take a little bit of getting used to for players from abroad, but with a year of experience in this country behind him, we should get the chance to see the real Pablo this season!

PAUL SCHARNER

POSITION: Midfielder

BIRTHDATE: 11/3/80

NATIONALITY: Austrian

ALBION APPEARANCES: 34

ALBION GOALS: 4

Albion's Austrian international certainly made a big impact in his first season at The Hawthorns, especially at the last home game against Everton when he dyed his hair blue and white! Paul played as Youssouf Mulumbu's defensive midfield partner for most of the season but he also had an important spell at centre-half – no big deal for a man who played every outfield position for his former club, Wigan Athletic!

YOUSSOUF MULUMBU

POSITION: Midfielder

BIRTHDATE: 25/1/87

NATIONALITY: Congolese

ALBION APPEARANCES: 74+12

ALBION GOALS: 10

If there's a more popular player at The Hawthorns than Youssouf these days, it's hard to think of him! His 'here, there and everywhere' style catches the eye week after week, as does the defensive midfielder's ability to get forward and score some amazing goals like the ones at Blackpool and Everton, or the cracker that saw ten-man Albion beat Villa for the first time in many a long year – Kaka never managed to do that!

GEORGE THORNE

POSITION: Midfielder

BIRTHDATE: 4/1/93

NATIONALITY: English

ALBION APPEARANCES: 0+2

ALBION GOALS: 0

18- year-old George Thorne made his Premier League debut in the final game of last season, coming on as Albion trailed 3-0, walking off at the end after playing his part in the comeback to 3-3. He has represented England at most youth levels and was withdrawn from the Under-20 World Cup squad in order to play his part in Albion's pre-season in America, giving Roy Hodgson a chance to look at this product of Albion's Academy.

CHRIS BRUNT

POSITION: Winger

BIRTHDATE: 14/12/84

NATIONALITY: Northern Irish

ALBION APPEARANCES: 133+24

ALBION GOALS: 30

The Albion captain, replacing Scott Carson last season, Brunty continues to be one of the most important players at The Hawthorns. A good leader of the team, a great creator of goals with that magical left foot, he can score plenty too, the most memorable being the three against the Liverpool clubs – that great free-kick at Goodison Park and those two brave penalties that saw us finally beat Liverpool in the Premiership at The Hawthorns!

GRAHAM DORRANS

POSITION: Midfielder

BIRTHDATE: 5/5/87

NATIONALITY: Scottish

ALBION APPEARANCES: 75+13

ALBION GOALS: 19

Last season was one to forget for the Albion midfielder who was the club's Player of the Season in the promotion winning campaign. A string of injuries meant he never really found the form we know he can, and just as he was starting to reach his best, scoring that great goal against West Ham United at The Hawthorns, another ankle injury stopped him in his tracks. It'll be better for Graham this year!

JAMES MORRISON

POSITION: Midfielder

BIRTHDATE: 25/5/86

NATIONALITY: Scottish

ALBION APPEARANCES: 93+24

ALBION GOALS: 13

Albion's Scottish international put his injury problems of the previous year behind him by playing a big part in the season of survival. He scored some of the most memorable goals of the season, especially the belter against Manchester United on New Year's Day, and then another special one against Birmingham City that combined both close control and a powerful finish. A regular for Scotland as well as the Baggies.

JEROME THOMAS

POSITION: Winger

BIRTHDATE: 23/3/83

NATIONALITY: English

ALBION APPEARANCES: 56+7

ALBION GOALS: 11

The former Arsenal and Charlton winger had another influential season as the Throstles secured their spot in the Premier League once again. Jerome adapted his game late in the season to bring a more defensive element to his football to help the side get some great late results under Roy Hodgson – his slide tackle is getting to be as good as his Cruyff turn these days!

SIMON COX

POSITION: Striker

BIRTHDATE: 28/4/87

NATIONALITY: Irish

ALBION APPEARANCES: 35+22

ALBION GOALS: 14

Simon enjoyed an incredible end to last season, winning Albion's Goal of the Season and the BBC's Goal of the Month prize for his wonder goal against Tottenham Hotspur, before collecting his first international caps for Ireland, celebrating by scoring in games against Northern Ireland and Italy. It was a well deserved reward for a player who constantly works hard at his game and always tries to improve – a lesson to us all!

SOMEN TCHOYI

POSITION: Winger/Striker

BIRTHDATE: 29/1/83

NATIONALITY: Cameroonian

ALBION APPEARANCES: 10+16

ALBION GOALS: 7

Somen is one of the most exciting – and most unpredictable – players that the Throstles have signed in a long, long time. With two good feet, he used them both to score amazing goals before Christmas against Newcastle and Everton, after his first two goals had come after goalkeepers dropped the ball at his feet at Leicester and Manchester United. And then there was the incredible hat-trick at Newcastle on the last day of the season to drag Albion back from 3-0 down to get a 3-3 draw.

MARC-ANTOINE FORTUNE

POSITION: Striker

BIRTHDATE: 2/7/81

NATIONALITY: French

ALBION APPEARANCES: 33+11

ALBION GOALS: 7

Marco came back to West Bromwich early last season after a season away at Celtic in the SPL and his strength and physical presence made him a big player for the Baggies, often alongside Peter Odemwingie. Fortune is not as prolific a scorer as Odemwingie, but he works extremely hard for the team and is a regular creator of goalscoring opportunities for other players in the side.

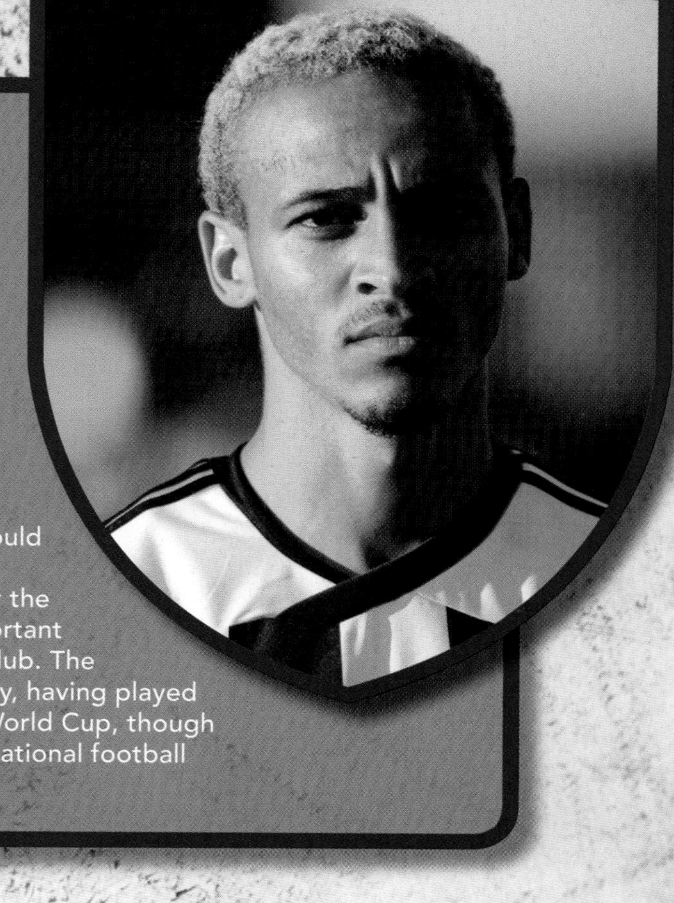

PETER ODEMWINGIE

POSITION: Striker

BIRTHDATE: 15/7/81

NATIONALITY: Nigerian

ALBION APPEARANCES: 29+3

ALBION GOALS: 15

The former Lokomotiv Moscow man could hardly have had a better first season in English football after he top scored for the Throstles, so many of them being important goals to win some key games for the club. The Nigerian is also a regular for his country, having played in both the Beijing Olympics and the World Cup, though he could have chosen to play his international football for Russia instead.

ISHMAEL MILLER

POSITION: Striker

BIRTHDATE: 5/3/87

NATIONALITY: English

ALBION APPEARANCES: 44+33

ALBION GOALS: 21

Ishmael Miller has had to endure two terrible years because of injuries, starting in December 2008 when he badly damaged his knee in a collision with Portsmouth goalkeeper David James. He went to QPR on loan early in 2011 in order to get some football and he will be looking to get his career back on course by becoming a regular in Roy Hodgson's Albion team over the course of this season.

Billy the Baggie

Albion gave themselves more competition at the back in the summer when they signed Billy Jones from Preston.

But while Billy is still a youngster, he brings plenty of experience to the dressing room – he's played over 300 games for Preston and Crewe already, as well as captaining England under 20s!

Roy Hodgson said, "We're really pleased we've been able to secure his signature in the face of stiff competition from other clubs for his services. It is great that he has chosen our club as the place to further his career and we are looking forward to working with him. We have been monitoring Billy's progress for some time and he has been a very consistent performer in the Championship for a long period. This is his chance to show he can be as good a player in the Barclays Premier League".

The 24-year-old Jones said "I'm made up to be here. It's bad for any player to be relegated, especially as Preston hadn't been relegated in 13 seasons from the Championship, so to then get news like this was great for me.

"I feel like I've improved year on year at Preston. I'm just glad the gaffer has seen that and I hope I can keep improving as a player at West Brom. I'm experienced in the Championship but the Premier League is a whole new league and different types of games.

"It's a fresh challenge, I'm still young and I'm really looking forward to hopefully cracking the Premier League. I feel playing in a team with better individuals is obviously going to improve me as a player. Hopefully I can just help the team out and prove myself in this league".

QUiz AnSweRs

WORDSEARCH, Page 17:

M	U	L	U	M	B	U	D	O	I	T
C	S	U	V	A	O	A	U	R	F	H
A	R	G	E	R	A	D	D	A	V	R
U	H	B	G	I	Z	N	O	Z	L	O
L	Q	R	Z	Q	Y	X	R	M	Y	S
E	K	E	O	K	O	B	R	U	N	T
Y	B	I	B	A	W	H	A	M	S	L
G	O	D	E	M	W	I	N	G	I	E
S	F	I	J	M	L	F	S	G	O	S
J	E	T	J	R	P	Y	C	T	U	E
B	A	G	G	I	E	B	I	R	D	Z

WHERE AM I?, Page 43:

THE BIG QUIZ, Page 26:

1. Manchester United
2. Lee Marshall v Leeds United (2002/3)
3. Joe Murphy v Liverpool (2002/3)
4. Igor Balis v Everton (2002/3)
5. Derek McInnes v Manchester United (2002/3)
6. Fulham
7. At Upton Park against West Ham
8. Gary Megson, Bryan Robson, Tony Mowbray, Roberto Di Matteo and Roy Hodgson. Frank Burrows and Michael Appleton have been caretaker managers
9. Robert Earnshaw and Somen Tchoyi
10. Earnshaw at Charlton (2004/5) and Tchoyi at Newcastle (2010/11)
11. 4-0 v Everton (2005/6)
12. 6-0 v Liverpool (2002/3) and 6-0 v Chelsea (2010/11)
13. Chris Brunt got both goals in the 2-1 win in 2010/11
14. Geoff Horsfield and Kieran Richardson
15. Youssouf Mulumbu
16. Carlos Vela v Wolves
17. Nwankwo Kanu and Darren Carter
18. Peter Odemwingie, Gonzalo Jara and Jerome Thomas
19. Everton, Birmingham and Sunderland
20. Peter Odemwingie v Sunderland

CROSSWORD, Page 48:

Across: 1 – Adidas; 5 – Hawthorns; 7 – Team; 8 – James; 11- Scharner; 13 – Myhill; 15 – Rochdale.

Down: 1 – Albion; 2 – Don; 3 – Shorey; 4 – Zoltan; 6 – Somen; 9 – Chris; 10 – Appleton; 11 – Simon Cox; 12 – Romania; 14 - Dutch

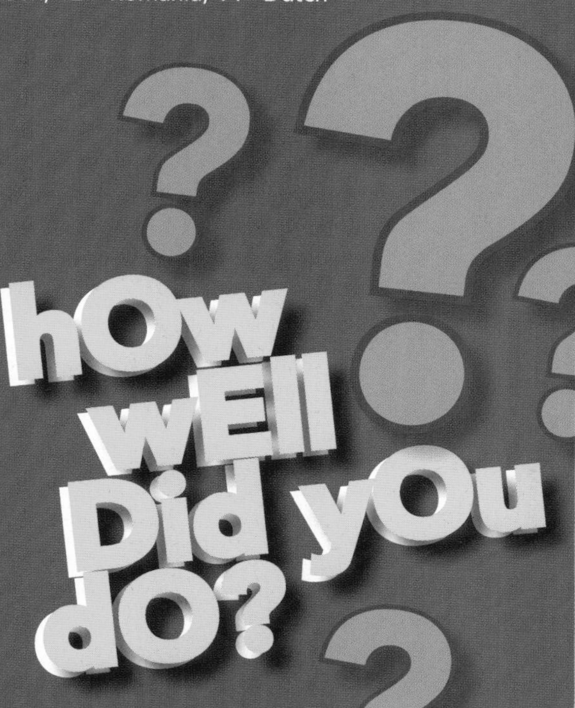

adidas
ALBION
博狗
bodog